UNDER THE MICROSCOPE

ELIZABETH CARR

THE USA'S FIRST IVF BABY

Bristol Books CIC, The Courtyard, Wraxall Hill,
Wraxall, Bristol BS48 1NA, United Kingdom

Under The Microscope
by Elizabeth Carr
Additional research by Martin Powell

Published by Bristol Books 2022
ISBN: 978-0-578-33702-9

ACKNOWLEDGEMENTS

Thanks are due to the following for supporting the production of this book:

Alan Scherer (cover photo)
Gina Andino (Brown Fertility)
Eric Flem (Nikon)
Laurent Christian Asker Melchior Tellier (Genomic Prediction)
Joe Burt (Bristol Books)
Staff of Empica PR, UK

To my Mom & Dad who fearlessly stepped into the unknown and who have been my biggest cheerleaders from the start.

Thank you Drs. Howard & Georgeanna Jones for tackling an incredible challenge during what should have been your retirement.

To my husband, Alan, for always pushing me to become my best self and seeing in me what I often lose sight of myself. And to my son, Trevor, for the unconditional zest for life and joy you bring to my life. I love you both endlessly.

And to the doctors, scientists, clinicians and warriors battling this thing called infertility: keep going. We need you.

CONTENTS

FOREWORD

In December 1981 Elizabeth Carr was the first person born through IVF in the USA. They called her a "test tube baby". She was in the spotlight from three cells old. Forty years on, she reflects on how being at the center of a scientific breakthrough has impacted on her life.

With additional historic context this book examines the issues that face those working on fertility and how the world reacts to scientific advancement.

BIOGRAPHIES

ELIZABETH CARR is a fearless patient advocate, striving to educate and empower people based on her life experiences and expertise within the fertility world.

Carr worked as a journalist at The Boston Globe for 15 years, first as a reporter, then in marketing and events.

She is a marathoner, journalist, triathlete, coffee connoisseur, wife and mother turned non-profit fundraising expert.

Elizabeth is the United States' first baby born from the in vitro fertilization procedure and the 15th in the world, which means she has been in the media spotlight since three cells old.

MARTIN POWELL is a UK-based journalist, author and historian. He wrote the biography of Louise Brown, the world's first test-tube baby, as a first-person account of her life in the spotlight. Published in 2015 it has sold worldwide, including being translated into Mandarin Chinese. Martin worked with Louise's mother, Lesley Brown, and has travelled to four continents with Louise and her family, handling worldwide media enquiries and meeting fertility scientists, doctors and patients.

He is a media specialist handling publicity for major corporates and businesses – mostly UK based. He is the author of four factual history books.

BEING NORMAL

Yes, I have a belly button.

Let's just get that out of the way right off the bat.

No, it's not the weirdest question I've been asked.

On December 28, 1981, I became the first baby born in the United States via in vitro fertilization (IVF). The infertility treatment was controversial at the time, and as yet untried in the United States, although there had been successes overseas years earlier with the birth of the world's first IVF baby, England's Louise Brown.

After my birth I was deemed by doctors to be a "normal, healthy, baby girl."

I've been working most of my life at that normal part. Maybe as a medical definition of a newborn, that description fit. But anyone who knows me, Elizabeth the person, well enough, knows better than to call me 'normal.'

Short? Sure. Loud? You bet. Terrible at math? That's me. But normal?

Normal kids don't watch NOVA documentaries of how their parents struggled to have a child, do they?

To outsiders, the fact that I have 10 giant volumes of scrapbooks documenting news articles written about my parents and stacks of VHS tapes and DVDs of my various television appearances may seem odd.

I have meticulously documented every bit of baby-babble my son has ever uttered (the very first was hi!), but I don't know what my first word was.

I don't have a baby book. Instead, I can tell you what my first headline read: "She's a cutie!" (There were countless others, of course, some not quite as flattering.)

The first time I realized I was not like everyone else was also the first time I watched that NOVA documentary - "A Daughter for Judy" - of my birth.

For all intents and purposes, it is my only "home movie," even though it went through months of filming, editing, and post-production.

The experience of watching it for the first time, however, was not like popping in home movies that make you nostalgic for past years. Instead, it was very much an experience where I can remember thinking that I was watching history unfold - not just my history - but also world history. And I was the one making the history simply through my existence.

I've seen the footage so many times now I have it memorized.

A young mother quietly walks beside her husband, cradling her tiny newborn daughter in her arms. The dark-haired trio takes their seats in front of hundreds of news reporters. Camera crews from local and overseas television and radio stations crowd around them. They don't seem overwhelmed by all the press, but instead are too busy gazing down at their daughter to look up in order for the photographers to get the perfect shot of the new family. The sound of constantly-clicking camera shutters is lulling the baby girl to sleep. She is two days old, and this will be her first - but not her last - press conference.

I don't remember that exact day because I was just a newborn.

However, I do remember the first time I watched that scene.

I watched it in a room full of doctors, reporters, and parents and children, who were part of the first batch of ten babies to come out of the clinic where I was born.

I was about five, sporting a bowl haircut, tights that I could never get to stay up, and black and white saddle shoes; a quintessential New England preppy, in miniature form.

When the film got to the part where my doctor, Dr. Howard Jones, announced my birth, I remember looking over at him from underneath my heavy bangs and smiling and then quickly looking back down at my shoes as if I needed to watch what was unfolding on the screen with some degree of reverence.

Even at that young age, I knew this wasn't something this doctor got to announce every day, with the entire world watching.

"This morning at 7:46, a daughter was born to Mrs. Judith Carr, a 28-year-old school teacher. The father is Mr. Roger Carr, a 30-year-old mechanical engineer," the footage of my doctor played.

I remember thinking there was no way that little baby was really me. Because I was just an average girl and, judging by all the fuss everyone was making, this baby on film was special: She was the first.

When the documentary was finished, I remember everyone in the screening room turning around to see my reaction.

That moment, when all those people turned around to look at me -that's when it happened. That's when I was asked the weirdest question I've ever been asked: What did I think of watching a documentary about my own birth?

For a 5-year-old such a question is pretty meta.

I remember vividly fidgeting in my seat between my pioneering doctors, and swinging my legs while I searched for a good answer.

What did I, a little girl who was the central character of this history-making event, think of herself?

Looking back on it now, I know there is no good way to answer such a bizarre question.

The adult in me, the not normal one with the outrageous sense of humor and tendency to go for big laughs, looking back on the incident, wants the five-year-old version of myself to shout ridiculous things like: "Where's my modeling contract?" or "What? No popcorn for this flick? Did we order the cheap seats?"

But the five-year-old one with the bowl cut and the bunchy tights didn't shout anything like that of course.

I think part of me must have known that everyone was looking for me to utter something poignant or profound about my own existence.

Every reporter in the room that day had their eyes trained on me; they noted every fidget, every giggle, and every blank stare on my face.

When it was over, I turned to my team of doctors who had surrounded me for the screening and answered that ridiculously meta question in the best way I knew how: with my own, simple question.

"Are all babies that slimy when they come out?"

Everyone laughed. Reporters scribbled furiously. It was, of course, the perfect quote.

Hell, it was almost normal.

What wasn't normal, of course, was the road my family had journeyed that led to my birth in the first place.

The road since then, well, that has been my own special type of normal, too.

But at least I own it.

MOM'S STORY

For years, the running joke in my family was what a media circus it was going to be when the day arrived that I had a child of my own.

We always joked about the headline: "Test-tube baby has test-tube baby of her own", because when I was younger I just assumed I was going to have a baby via IVF, because to me, that was the way families were created.

The truth was, my own fertility was not nearly as complicated as my mother's. I had my son without the help of any fertility treatments when I was 28-years-old.

Actually, looking back, her fertility wasn't that complicated either, compared to what some couples endure.

My mother always relays the story of the beginning of her infertility issues this way: she was in a gym class and her lower stomach felt awful.

My mother's gym teacher, not wanting to seem weak or too kind-hearted, told my mother she could go see the school nurse only after she ran a lap around the field before heading in. My mother, being a rule-follower, did so, but was doubled over in pain once she made it to the school nurse.

My mother's appendix was the issue.

She had surgery to remove her appendix, and she didn't think about that day in gym class again until years later when she was trying to start a family with my father.

Apparently, the appendix surgery caused some scarring that complicated her fertility options.

According to a study done in 1986, years after I was born, women who had ruptured appendixes had up to a five times greater risk of suffering from tubal infertility, in which a woman's fallopian tubes are damaged.

So, every time my mother got pregnant, the pregnancy would result in a tubal or ectopic pregnancy, which means the fertilized egg doesn't attach to the lining of the uterus like it is supposed to.

My mother had three ectopic pregnancies and her fallopian tubes were basically blown up and not functioning properly. Eventually, both of her fallopian tubes were surgically removed.

After severe internal bleeding that caused her to be rushed by ambulance to the closest hospital and the largest scare of my parents' marriage, my mother's OB-GYN told her that, essentially, she would never have biological children of her own.

Devastated, my parents began to investigate other options: not being parents just wasn't part of their plan – they wanted a family – their family.

One day, after a follow up check-up, my mother's OB-GYN pulled out a brochure from a conference he had attended which mentioned a procedure called in vitro fertilization. While not performed in the United States yet, the procedure had enjoyed success in England with the birth of Louise Joy Brown in 1979 as the world's first IVF baby.

The OB-GYN told my mother maybe she should research the procedure, and see what she could find out. Asking her doctor to write a recommendation letter to the IVF program in Norfolk,

Virginia, my mother quickly heard that she'd been accepted.

On April 17 – my mother's 28th birthday – a fertilized egg was implanted after the clinic doctors and staff sang her a round of "Happy Birthday."

A few weeks later, my mother's latest pregnancy test confirmed she was, in fact, pregnant.

Because IVF was illegal in Massachusetts at the time, where my parents were living, they made regular flights down to Virginia for check-ups.

And, because an IVF pregnancy in France had ended in miscarriage after much media attention, my parents' identities were kept quiet. Dr. Howard Jones announced during a press conference that there was a pregnancy, but said personal details about the couple would be kept secret.

An entire wing of the hospital was closed off for my parents, and only essential personnel were allowed access. All those essential personnel were given badges and the tightly held secret was named "Operation Santa Claus."

So that my father could come and go from the hospital as he needed, he was given a fake name, so that the press outside the hospital would not know his true identity. They were also given a fake description of him. He was given the name "Roger Dalton" - taking my mother's maiden name instead of using his own last name.

Armed guards stood outside my mother's hospital door as well, as a double precaution.

During the last month of pregnancy, my parents rented a condo in Virginia Beach, since they were slated to deliver via c-section just a few days after Christmas 1981.

On December 28, 1981, I arrived, on time and perfectly healthy.

A MOM WHO CHANGED THE WORLD

When Elizabeth was born at 7.46am on December 28, 1981, by caesarian section it vindicated the work of the fledgling IVF program in the US, which had been underway for just 21 months.

Women like Judith Carr, just a regular 28-year-old schoolteacher from Westminster, Massachusetts, were finding out about this new technique, which worldwide had only existed successfully for three-and-a-half years.

Some of the comments to the media when Operation Santa Claus came to a successful conclusion with the delivery of five-pound 12 ounce Elizabeth show just how suspicious people were of what was happening. The terminology, even by the doctors, betrayed their awe and disbelief that it had actually worked and a need to demonstrate to the public that all was normal.

First Dr Mason Andrews, who performed the ceasarian said: "The baby cried right away and that was very reassuring. It was a relief to know this was a normal baby. The baby had her first feeding and, doctors said, took an ounce of formula very well."

Dr Andrews, who was then 62 and vice Mayor of Norfolk, was very proud of the city and the fact it was at the forefront of medical science.

Even Howard Jones was far from bullish about the success, saying: "I think this is a day of hope" and saying it offered the "possibility of childbirth" to approximately 600,000 American women who had damaged or missing fallopian tubes. A huge understatement of the difference that IVF was about to make to the world.

But perhaps they had in mind the views of the Rev Jerry

Falwell of Lynchburg, Virginia. He was a respected Southern Baptist Pastor and televangelist, who just two years before had co-founded the Moral Majority.

The Moral Majority was the most prominent political lobbying organization at the time on behalf of the Christian Right and Republican Party and certainly had a big following. The Rev Falwell said that the scientists were "delving into an area that is far too sacred for human beings to be involved in."

There was a moral tightrope to be walked by those working to help people overcome fertility problems through science. Dr Andrews had said it was "almost immoral" not to help people with fertility problems if it was scientifically possible.

With the birth of Elizabeth, IVF had circled the globe, with successes in the UK, Australia and USA.

At least 63 other women were pregnant across the world through IVF when Elizabeth was born. Success rates had risen to around one in 10 in the first clinics and were improving all the time.

One of the pregnancies was reported at the University of California Medical Center and the University of Texas Health Science Center in Houston had also stated they were working on making IVF babies. The IVF baby boom was about to begin in America, enabling couples who previously had no chance the opportunity to have a family.

JOURNALIST

Many people go through life trying to figure out exactly what they want to do for a living. I have always known, as if nothing else made sense.

I have always wanted to write. Always wanted to tell stories.

I remember the exact moment I knew I wanted to be a journalist. I was in 8th grade. The newsmagazine 'Focus' sent two women journalists over to write a profile of the first IVF baby in the United States now that she was a pre-teen.

My parents and I had been down this road before. We figured it would be the same routine it always was: host the writers for a few days, give them a snapshot of what our life was like, answer some silly questions, pose for silly photos and they'd be on their way.

But it wasn't like that at all.

The writer lived in Germany and wrote for a German magazine, but was born in France and spoke impeccable English. She asked questions in English, took notes in French and then translated them into German.

She was gorgeous and brilliant.

She asked insightful questions and had what seemed like the most glamorous job in the world to me.

The photographer the magazine sent over was from California. She had long blonde hair, didn't shave and had photographed war zones. And here she was, this award-winning photographer, taking photos of me in the barren wintertime of New England and shooting me with the same zeal I imagined she would have photographing the Queen of England.

Together they were a force to be reckoned with - and I was fascinated.

They spent a few weeks with my family and I.

Maggie, the photographer, took me rock climbing for the first time, while Anna taught me the perfect way to tie a silk scarf around my neck and make it look flawless - as if it took no effort at all.

They were the first writers who really took the time to get to know me; they didn't just ask their questions and get their answers. They watched my behavior, met my friends, saw me cry.

After the first week, I came to realize they knew me better than most of my close friends did.

It made me want to know people the way they knew me. I wanted that job. I wanted to know people on a level so intimate that I could just look at them and have an idea of what a certain intonation or movement meant.

So, I started to interview my interviewers. What kind of schooling did you need to become a journalist? Why do you love it? Why do you hate it? Where have you been? What have you seen?

When they had enough material to file their story about me, they packed up and left. And while they weren't friends, I couldn't help but think that it was sad to know these powerful, amazing women were exiting my life and I would likely never see them again – and I never did.

That was one of the best experiences I had as a child in the spotlight. But there were terrible times, too.

There were times people wrote things that weren't true about me; times ugly words were printed about my family; times I wanted to crawl in a hole and curl up and not see the light of day because of photographs an awkward, pre-teen girl should never see printed or blown up on printed pages.

And yet, that's my life. From day one it's been documented.

In a way, it's hard to imagine that I would have a career as anything other than a journalist. What else would a product of the media do?

It is as if I cannot separate myself from the media considering it has been a part of my life since before I was born.

Growing up, I was protected from the media by very savvy parents and a hospital media team that carefully suggested which interviews I should do with which media outlets.

We declined interviews with things we didn't see as educational, and carefully picked who we'd allow to tell our story.

I learned quite young the difference (in my mind) between a careful reporter and skilled writer and those who are concerned with nothing more than getting something - anything - down on paper.

Other times, things cut me to the core. There's something so final, so real about seeing something about your life printed. It's especially hurtful if it's made up and wrong.

It is one thing dealing with hurtful words in the comfort of your own home, with your parents beside you to tell you it doesn't matter what other people say.

It is, however, a very different beast when you see hurtful words when you are out grocery shopping with your college roommate. There is nowhere to hide. No one to cry to. You are alone, but in a very public space.

It was one of those nights: the kind of night where we

didn't want go out out, but we didn't really want to stay in. The compromise, of course, was heading to Star Market to buy macaroni and cheese to make in our dorm room. We'd stuff our faces with fake processed cheese product over noodles and then watch movies until the wee hours of the morning.

It was one of our favorite things to do.

Only, on this pilgrimage, as we stood in line trying to figure out if we had enough cash or if we had to bust out our ATM cards, we both saw a familiar face on the tabloid racks in the checkout line. My roommate spotted it a half a second before I did.

"Oh my god, E, is that you?" she asked.

She had that tone I hated. That half-excited, half-shocked, tone. It was a tone I grew up hearing, usually accompanied by the question disguised as a statement: "you're the first Test-tube baby in the United States?"

Sigh.

Here we go, I thought.

"Oh my god, this is so cool," my roommate went on to say. "You're in a tabloid. A legit tabloid."

"Great," I said, half annoyed and half exhausted by the idea.

"They didn't interview me, you know," I told my companion. "And half of the stuff in here is totally wrong," I said, pointing to a table comparing myself and the first test-tube baby in the world, Louise Brown.

"I know," my roommate said. "But you're in a TABLOID! I have to buy it," she said.

"Please don't," I said flatly.

"You can sign it!" my roommate said. I rolled my eyes at that idea.

I pulled out my cash to buy the mac and cheese while she pulled out her cash to buy the tabloid. As she silently tucked it under her arm for our walk back to the dorm, we walked in silence.

It was odd knowing that the girl I was sharing a room with had a piece of paper she was going to read that was supposedly about my life. Why couldn't she just ask me whatever it was she thought she was going to learn from three paragraphs in a tabloid?

I never did sign it for her.

JOURNALISTS & IVF

Journalists, and their interpretation of science, have shaped the way that IVF and fertility issues have been presented to the world – sometimes for good and sometimes for bad.

It has not always been the big-hitting national media outlets or the influential science journals that have had the biggest effect. There are two things that all journalists have that are common.

One is a need to explain things simply so their audience can understand it – which means often the subtle nuances of scientists and medical professionals get lost in translation. Secondly, a desire to balance the report with some opposition – so no matter how much something seems to be a benefit to mankind they will look for someone to oppose it.

Journalists were interested in the story of Elizabeth Carr long before she was even conceived. It has all the ingredients for a great news yarn. It is a story about babies, who are universally cute and loveable; it is controversial with religious and political issues; and her birth was a first, so at the time a unique event.

Peter Harris, Medical Correspondent of the Manchester Evening News in the UK, has to be mentioned. He interviewed Patrick Steptoe, the gynecologist, about his work in a clinic in Oldham in the 1970s.

Given a lot of information about attempts to make a baby "in vitro" he thought that his readers were unlikely to be keen on Latin phrases meaning "in glass" and needed a handier reference phrase – he came up with "test tube baby". He claims he asked Mr Steptoe if that was a reasonable description and Steptoe must have shrugged or couldn't think of anything better – and so a phrase was born.

It was soon picked up by the British national press and imported to America as a ready-made description of this new technique. Of course, the fact that no test tubes were used was by-the-by!

Faced with little in the way of illustration other than some folks in white coats peering into microscopes, the newspaper illustrators got to work and soon lots of drawings and cartoons of fully formed babies in test tubes were adorning the pages of newspapers and magazines. As most people just read the headlines and look at the pictures it meant plenty of confusion for the public over exactly what was happening here.

Much of that confusion led to Elizabeth Carr being asked some dumb questions later in life about her perceived incubation period in the test tube.

As early as 1965 journalists were having an influence on how this story would be perceived. Bob Edwards, who eventually got a Nobel Prize for his work, sent an article to the prestigious medical publication The Lancet, only to be told that the editor could see little point in his work.

They eventually accepted a cut-down version of his work to date in curing infertility. It was picked up by the UK national newspaper The Sunday Times under a heading "Births May Be By Proxy" and the story said they were "experiments reminiscent of Aldous Huxley's Brave New World".

The 1930s science fiction novel outlining a dystopian world where scientific advancement is used to make people conform to the State got a lot of mentions in a lot of articles in the early days of IVF. They made for exciting reading but irritated people like Edwards and Howard Jones as they were based on the assumption that all scientific advances would be used for some ill.

A 1970 television documentary into the pioneering work led to headlines such as "Babies Storm Growing" (Daily Express); "Test Tube Babies Raise Moral Issues" (Daily Telegraph) and even "Ban The Test Tube Baby" (Sun) and "Move to Threshold of Genetic Engineering" (The Times).

In 1978 Time Magazine in New York devoted eight pages to the subject, including a cartoon of two children playing with a chemistry set with the caption: "They are playing mothers and fathers" and a front page that aped the creation mural in the Sistine Chapel in Rome with a test tube at the heart of it. Journalists just loved to stir the religious and moral argument.

One journalist interview in 1978 did have an amazing effect and led directly to Elizabeth's birth. Howard Jones was moving to Norfolk, Virginia, on the very day that Louise Brown was born. A reporter from the local newspaper tracked him down and he sat on packing cases and chatted to her as she was keen to get his reaction to events in the UK.

One question she asked was whether it was possible to carry out the same technique in Virginia. He said it was. She asked what was the biggest barrier? He replied "money" as the research needed more funding.

The next day the newspaper carried the story and a grateful former patient of Georgeanna Jones, who had been successful in life, rang to ask just how much was needed.

The funds were duly donated enabling Georgeanna and Howard to assemble a team of young scientists to carry out pioneering in vitro fertilization work at the Eastern Virginia Medical School, leading to the birth of Elizabeth just a couple of years later. A great example of when a journalist's input made a real difference to the advance of the science.

Of course, a picture is worth a thousand words and it was no accident when Life magazine sat a diaper-clad baby Elizabeth on a laboratory bench in November 1982 for her cover shot!

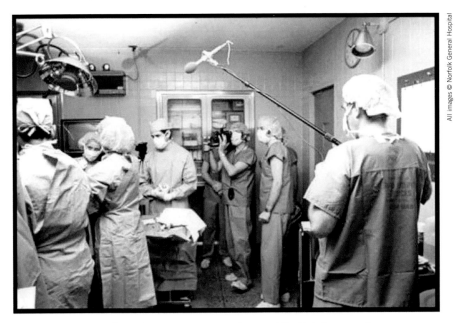

The delivery room was filled with a camera crew to document the historic moment.

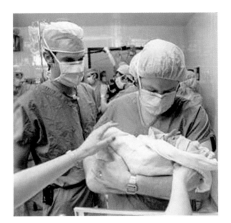

Roger Carr holding his daughter for the first time.

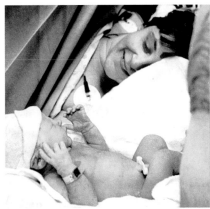

Elizabeth, Judy & Roger in the delivery room on the day she was born.

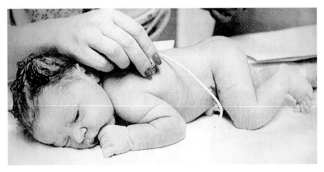

Elizabeth is checked out by doctors after she arrived on Dec. 28, 1981.

Judy laughs during Elizabeth's first press conference at three days old.

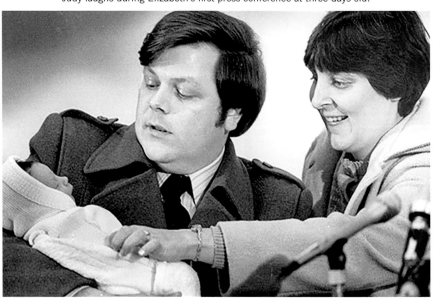

Roger, Judy & Elizabeth at a press conference once they arrived home from Virginia where Elizabeth was born.

Roger & Judy enjoying their toddler at their home in Westminster, Massachusetts.

Elizabeth, Roger & Judy appearing on a television show to celebrate another birthday.

A typical toddler, Elizabeth smiles during a summer vacation.

What is it that makes **Elizabeth Carr special?**

A specially produced handout explaining IVF to prospective parents that featured Elizabeth on the cover.

All staff involved in caring for Elizabeth's parents wore this special patch. VIP stood for "Vital Impregnation Program"

Elizabeth on her 10th birthday.

Roger, Judy & Elizabeth sit for a formal family portrait on her 10th birthday.

A quiet moment on vacation with Roger & Elizabeth.

Elizabeth in front of a Christmas tree when she was celebrating her 8th birthday.

Elizabeth and her mother, Judy, reading at home.

Elizabeth and her parents on her 10th birthday in front of the Life Magazine cover she graced as a baby.

A family vacation in quiet Bar Harbor, Maine atop Cadillac Mountain.

Judy & Roger celebrating their 35th anniversary on a cruise.

Elizabeth and her mother, Judy, when she graduated from high school.

Bar Harbor, Maine, was the annual family vacation spot every summer.

A family vacation in quiet Bar Harbor, Maine. Pictured left to right: Judy, Alan (Elizabeth's husband) Elizabeth, Roger, Trevor (Elizabeth's son) and Chase, the family dog.

Elizabeth in 2010 when she was pregnant with her son, Trevor.

In 2010, Elizabeth became a mother herself, giving birth to her son, Trevor.

Elizabeth with her family in the backyard of their home in New Hampshire. Left to right: Alan, Trevor, Elizabeth.

Elizabeth at home in New Hampshire.

Elizabeth at home in New Hampshire.

Photographed in her diaper to grace the cover of Life Magazine in 1982.

U.S. News featuring Elizabeth.

The Newsday Magazine featuring Elizabeth.

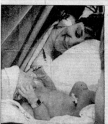

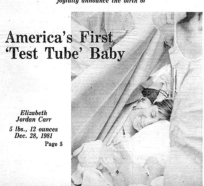
Media from the day of Elizabeth's birth.

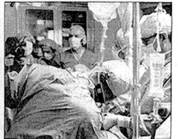
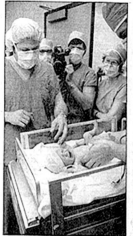
A television review of the NOVA documentary featuring Elizabeth called "A Daughter for Judy".

Elizabeth meeting neonatologist Dr. Fred Wirth for the first time in 2004.

Dr. Howard Jones, Elizabeth & Judy, during a get together in Norfolk, Virginia.

Elizabeth's birth is cemented in history. She was even a question on the popular gameshow "jeopardy" and finally met Louise Brown - the world first - from the UK on stage at the Midwest Reproductive Symposium International in Chicago.

IN 1981 ELIZABETH
CARR BECAME
THE USA's FIRST
OF THESE BABIES,
WITH LESS FANFARE
THAN THE ONE
ACROSS THE POND

All of the Jones Institute babies were gathered with their parents for a photo when Elizabeth was seven.

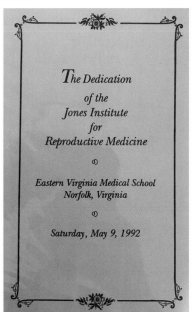

The Dedication
of the
Jones Institute
for
Reproductive Medicine

❁

Eastern Virginia Medical School
Norfolk, Virginia

❁

Saturday, May 9, 1992

The program for the dedication of the Jones Institute of Reproductive Medicine.

JONES INSTITUTE DEDICATION AND MOTHER'S DAY
C E L E B R A T I O N

After a week's worth of steady rain, Mother Nature cooperated and provided sunny skies for the Jones Institute Dedication and Mother's Day Celebration. More than 800 people from Hampton Roads and around the country spent the weekend at EVMS to attend the Dedication Ceremony for the new Jones building May 9 and to celebrate Mother's Day May 10.

Number one meets number one thousand: Ten-year-old Elizabeth Carr, the first Jones IVF baby, holds Allison Evangelista, the 1,000th Jones baby, born February 11.

The Dedication Ceremony was just the beginning of the festivities. An outdoor "Wild West Supper Barbecue" was held Saturday evening on the lawn of Smith-Rogers Hall, and on Sunday, Jones families gathered at the Norfolk Marriott Waterside for brunch. Here are some highlights of that special weekend captured by photographer Nute Nicholson.

Be a part of the new Jones Institute building.
Honor a loved one with an inscribed courtyard brick
and
enjoy scenes of the Jones Dedication weekend in the new facility
with the purchase of a 30-minute video tape. *Details inside.*

For many years, all of the babies born at the Jones Institute in Norfolk, Virginia would get together for Mother's Day. Here, Elizabeth is pictured with babies 1,000 and 1,001 in 1992.

Elizabeth sits on the lap of Dr. Howard Jones during a trip to New York City that the family and the doctor took in order to appear on Good Morning America and Today.

Through the years, Elizabeth has lent her voice to the infertility community, striving to educate all about fertility treatments.

Elizabeth giving a speech during a RESOLVE function.

Elizabeth and members of RESOLVE pose for a photo during a walk to raise funds for advocacy work.

Elizabeth poses with fellow advocates during a "Night of Hope" gala event hosted by RESOLVE, the national infertility association.

Elizabeth with the Nikon microscope that took her first photo at three cells old.

An old Nikon ad, featuring Elizabeth & Dolly the cloned sheep.

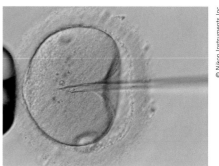

IVF photos captured with a Nikon microscope.

NUMBERS

I own a heart-shaped sterling silver necklace with the number "1" on one side, and my initials on the other.

I only wear it on special occasions - like a mini good-luck charm - or I wear it when I go to Virginia to visit the doctors who made me possible.

It is a kind of silent reminder of my roots. I've often wondered if the other nine children from my clinic who also have one feel the same way.

Some of the children, from the moment we were gifted the pendants at a Mother's Day reunion, have never removed the symbol from around their necks. Others have tucked the small charms away. For the rest, like me, it's not something I hide, but even the act of wearing it means more explaining than I'd like to do when first meeting someone.

For the longest time, my number-necklace was my identifier among that one specific peer group: The group of nine other first "test tube" babies.

I am, of course, the oldest. Number 10 is two years younger.

For the longest time, when this group of 10 "babies" got together, we referred to each other by our numbers rather than our names. "Me and two and three are going to the mall," I remember saying to my parents when I was 13. "Six and eight weren't sure if they were coming, but can you tell them where I'll be if they come looking?"

I have often wondered if we fell into this act of going by our numbers because it made us feel like part of some elite club, or simply because it was safe, familiar, and a way of sharing our common thread without actually talking about our conception.

The numbers became our shorthand.

Although we 10 were - and some still are - close (almost like brothers and sisters) none of us, to my knowledge have ever discussed the fact that we were born via IVF with each other. I can't tell if it is because we feel like we don't need to, or because, on some level, we don't want to.

And yet, it is our common experience that brings us together - the one thing you would think we would discuss - or at least jump from as a starting point. We have never talked about having newspaper articles written about us - not because we did something spectacular or ground-breaking but instead simply because we came into the world like other children do every day.

Nor have we discussed our fears about whether infertility would ever be something we'd have to face ourselves, as our parents before us faced, or how we will tell our children our place in reproductive history.

It is as if the sheer act of having a number attached to our persona allows us to at once never discuss, but also completely understand, all our questions, concerns, and struggles.

We all have different stories, brought together by one common thread. We all have numbers. Some are just higher or lower than others.

When I was 10, I got to meet, and hold, babies 1,000 and 1,001. They were twins. I remember their parents telling me "without you and your parents, our babies wouldn't be here."

Being 10, I remember just giggling and saying how cute the babies were. But, I also remember thinking how overwhelming it was to be a kind of role model for these tiny babies, who were now connected to me by default and through no choice of their own.

They were simply born into those numbers 1,000 and 1,001.

Would they grow up to take comfort in their numbers as I had, I wondered? Would their parents one day show them the photograph of baby 1 holding them?

Who would answer these baby's unspoken questions - the ones I was sure they were bound to have when they were old enough to ponder where babies came from?

That was when I realized these babies may not have the same concerns or struggles we first 10 did, because with 1,001 IVF births from one clinic alone (forget the hundreds more that were cropping up across the country), I realized IVF was becoming "normal."

And yet, all these years later, I cannot recall the names of those twin babies. So maybe it's not that "normal" after all.

Even now, I recall only their numbers.

NUMBERS ADD UP!

Trying to give children born through IVF a number today would be an impossible task with the rate of births ticking up faster than the price counter on a pump at a gas station.

In reality nobody is counting any longer and as soon as you say a figure for IVF births in the world it is out of date by the time you write it down. But it all started out fairly slowly.

Elizabeth has two numbers – number one in the US and also number 15 in the world. She was born three years and five months after Louise Brown, so at her birth date you could count the babies born in a year on one hand.

The second IVF baby announced by pioneers Edwards and Steptoe – Alastair MacDonald – was born in Scotland in January 1979. His mother, Grace, was already pregnant when Louise was born through the same program.

Just 67 days after Louise Brown was born Indian scientist and physician Subhash Mukhopadhyay produced Kanupriya Agarwal, known as Durga, who many now believe was the second in the world, but the scientist faced great opposition in his own country and committed suicide in 1981.

Lesley Brown, Louise's mother, became the first woman in the world to have a second IVF baby in June 1982. Baby Natalie was number 40 in the world, so it was running at an average of 10 a year at that time.

In the early 1980s there were pioneers all around the world working on the technique in their own territories and all of them knew each other and shared information. Howard Jones in the USA and Robert Edwards in the UK had shared information for years but there were significant contributions from Alan Trounson

(Australia), Lars Hamberger (Sweden) and Jean Cohen (France).

The pioneer names that are remembered today tend to be the ones who had some success. Many others were also working on aspects of IVF without great breakthroughs but their work enabled the science to develop.

The way the numbers rose is perfectly illustrated by the statistics from Australia. In 1980 there was one baby born in Australia through IVF; in 1981 it was 11; in 1982 there were 30 more and in 1983 there were 97.

Not only was the science improving but various barriers were being knocked down around the world as people came to terms with the fact that "test tube babies" were the same as any other baby – they just needed a little science to help them get here.

Not only were the pioneers working on perfecting the technique in the laboratory, they were working hard in overcoming ethical and legal issues. Many religious groups feared scientists might be "playing God" and even in the very early days the potential for the technique to be used by same-sex couples was recognized and that was controversial.

People feared the children born would have disabilities or other medical problems, but with every success the pressure eased; governments started to tackle the legal issues and set laws for this new technique and that allowed more and more babies to be born.

In the 21st century it is probably better to talk about children born through Assisted Reproductive Technology (ART) rather than IVF as so many other techniques have been added to the pantheon of ways to help people with fertility issues.

The International Committee Monitoring Assisted Reproductive Technology (ICMART) is an independent body which looks at global trends in the area from established and reliable sources.

By 2016 they were reporting that there were 6.5 million people in the world born through ART techniques by 2018 their best estimate was more than eight million with around half a million babies born every year.

China had rules for decades that couples could only have a single baby, so that meant ART in that country wasn't encouraged, although China's first IVF baby was born in 1988. But once that rule was dropped IVF clinics sprang up and in 2016 it was reported that 900,000 cycles were performed; more than in Japan or USA.

So, it seems that from Elizabeth's days of knowing people born with single digit or double-digit numbers in the pecking order – any baby born today is likely to have a number with eight digits in it – that would require a big heart pendant on that necklace!

A SENSE OF PLACE

Ever have places you just could not live?

I spent a day with a colleague in NYC. We were covering a running apparel fashion show. I commented many times to my colleague that I could "never live in NYC."

Not because I don't like the city, but because I have rough associations with it – namely every time I had to make a big television appearance growing up as an IVF spokesbaby (yes, I made that term up) my parents and I had to travel to NYC.

I remember going in December, right around my birthday, to appear on 'Good Morning America.'

I was about 10 at the time. The TV show put us up in a fancy hotel. A car picked us up and whisked us away in the morning to the studio. I got my makeup done by the studio stylist. I remember she put foundation on my "too-pale for TV" father and she told my mother she had "cheekbones to die for."

A comedian who was waiting to go on before me rubbed my face and told me I was "precious". I remember thinking TV was really, really weird.

The camera guys told me never to become a TV journalist. "And even worse if you work behind the camera!"

We sat on uncomfortable vinyl furniture and I answered

the normal round of "do you feel normal? Do you feel special?" questions. I hated those questions.

When my parents and I arrived home from our trip, there was a light blinking on our answering machine. It was the booking agent for the "Today" show.

"Saw you on GMA, and we simply MUST have you on," she explained.

I didn't want to go.

We went back to NYC and Katie Couric interviewed me. I was asked the same round of questions. Those questions – probing to see if I was a "normal" kid – just made me cringe inside. My parents knew I hated it.

We saw Diane Keaton eating one table over from us at a French restaurant that night. We had a fancy dessert (or at least my 10-year old brain thought it was fancy).

And I remember thinking I just wanted to go home. Back to where people didn't ask me if I was normal. Where it wasn't crowded on the sidewalks. Where people didn't put makeup on me. Where it was just me, Mom, Dad, and the dog.

It's not NYC's fault, but after the apparel fashion show, I felt the same sense of relief when we left the city as I did when I was 10. I guess you never outgrow some things.

WORLD TRAVELS

Awkward questions about IVF are not confined to New York. The same curiosity that prompted the uncomfortable feeling that Elizabeth had at the hands of "Good Morning America" and the "Tonight Show" is still felt by many undergoing assistance to have a baby.

Of course, in the USA and many other countries where IVF is well-established, the debate and style of questions has moved on. Basic IVF techniques are well-established, generally accepted and understood.

Since Elizabeth's birth IVF has become established all over the world. Sub-Saharan Africa is generally said to be the area with the fewest IVF clinics compared to worldwide but even there it is fast growing – and needs to be to meet the demand.

It is an area where infection-related tubal damage is the commonest cause of infertility. In many of the African cultures there is a social stigma associated with childlessness which makes it even more crucial that people get help.

In these areas the questions about whether an IVF baby is a normal baby still dominate the media coverage. Clinics are now well-established in many African countries and one of the main battles those clinics face is answering this curiosity.

African conferences of IVF experts are now well-established as are help groups for couples seeking fertility support, so that they can get the facts to help them make decisions.

The media questioning in the USA is now more likely to be focused on the leading edge techniques. Egg and embryo freezing, sperm donation and scientific breakthroughs involving gene manipulation and editing DNA are major targets.

In truth this spotlight of questioning is vitally needed in an area where science rubs so closely up against moral, religious and ethical views. One of the most fascinating things about the whole story of IVF and reproductive medicine is that it has always been running ahead of the lawmakers.

Just because a technique for making babies is possible does that mean it should be allowed? Is the world ready for every breakthrough that scientists can make?

The curiosity of the media is understandable and is part of the process that eventually leads to the scientific breakthroughs coming into law. The South Africa surgeon Christiaan Barnard, who carried out the first heart transplant back in 1967, faced similar criticism and yet now organ transplants are relatively routine and unremarkable to the media.

It is interesting to note the difference in attitude to the procedure at the time by Barnard and the media. There are no pictures of that first heart going into the recipient, Mr Washkansky. That is because Barnard, who had successfully carried out the routine before on dogs, felt it wasn't that big a deal to have a photo. The media later offered $1 million for a photo!

Mr Barnard discarded the rubber gloves he used for the operation in the trash as usual – a newspaper offered to buy them a few days later for $25,000. It is largely forgotten now that the transplant program went ahead despite the fact that Mr Washkansky died 18 days after the operation. An autopsy showed that nothing in the operation had contributed to his death from pneumonia, but there was much speculation in the media and invention of a new phenomena which they called "transplant lung" with claims that it was all part of his body rejecting the new heart.

Every medical breakthrough in history has been scrutinized by the media on behalf of the public and as boundaries are pushed back and new discoveries made there will always be those awkward questions.

What will always be difficult will be the "case studies" at every new breakthrough. People like Elizabeth and Mr Washkansky are the human face of the scientific breakthroughs.

Many of the questions Elizabeth and her family faced were unfair and impossible to answer. The Big Apple journalists were really directing them at the wrong people.

But it is the human story that will always grab the attention of the media. Those at the leading edge, wherever they are in the world, need to appreciate the pressure that this might bring on the families thrust into the media spotlight.

LUCKY PENNY

We were young – I'll say 10, she'll argue and say 13 – when we found it.

I met Jamie when I was seven, at a sleep away camp in the woods of Maine. We were in the same cabin, and I think that first year she was on the top bunk and I was on the bottom (later, we'd always have to have top bunks next to or across from each other, but never the same because it was too hard to talk after the lights went out that way).

In the summer, there were four of us: Alex, Rachel, Jamie, and me. Every summer, all four of us would spend six weeks away from our parents. We'd sail, swim, hike, gossip about who the cute boys in the oldest boys cabin were, and make friendship bracelets, hair wraps and various things made of that mysterious plastic rope known as gimp.

The four of us were a force, and each had our role. I was the loud one (shocker). Jamie was the one who wanted to save the world. Rachel was the cool one. Alex was the smart one. We were more than that, of course, and together we filled in each other's gaps.

Through the years; through boyfriends and babies, we've all remained friends.

Jamie and I, though, have also always had this penny.

On school breaks, and in between writing letters to each other, we'd visit. She'd bus down from Maine, or my mother would drive me up. I lived with her family one summer when I was a camp counselor at a day camp, and I wouldn't have missed her Bat Mitzvah for the world.

On one of these school year visits, we found this penny. It was lying face up, which, we decided, meant it was CLEARLY lucky. Not to mention, it had a mish-mash of our birthdays on it – my birth month (December) and her birth year (1982).

Even. More. Lucky.

We concocted a plan: we would have joint ownership over the penny. And we'd pass it back and forth whenever the other person either needed luck, or when we'd see each other again.

The penny has seen some mileage. It was sent by post. It has been hand carried. It spent nearly a year glued to a piece of paper at the bottom of a box where I kept all my camp pen pal letters.

As we got older, we got more savvy about the penny, constructing a holder for it out of plastic. Inside the white holder with magenta thread, that penny would not budge.

When Jamie got married, I gave her husband the penny, telling him he'd never be forgiven if, after 20+ years of friendship it was lost. I think I sufficiently scared him.

What we've discovered, over the years, is not that the penny has luck. Surely it is *just* a penny.

What matters is that Jamie and I discovered, at a young age, that you create your own luck.

You just have to be willing to see it.

LUCKY CHARMS & FERTILITY

The birth of Elizabeth Carr marked the end of hundreds – no, probably thousands - of years – of good luck symbols associated with fertility.

Her own lucky penny gave general luck but there is hardly an archaeological dig in the world that hasn't produced some kind of object that the experts have then declared to be a "fertility" symbol.

Whether it is symbols representing the goddess Inanna in the Royal Cemetery of Ur in Iraq from ancient Mesopotamia; charms representing Isis the goddess of motherhood of fertility in ancient Egypt or the 28,000 year old phallus found in Hohle Fels, a cave in Bavaria, Germany, it seems you can't look into the past without finding something to do with fertility.

Elizabeth's birth and the work of the pioneers of IVF brought science to bear where previously many women and men who had not managed to conceive had to rely on religion, lucky charms, rituals, strange foods and odd behaviour in the hope and belief that it would end their search for a child.

When the Dionne quintuplets were born in Canada in 1934 thousands of people bought lucky stones to help them conceive. These were basically from a pile of rocks close to where the girls were living – the theory being that the "fertility stones" must be lucky as they had been so close to such a miracle birth that they might help others to conceive.

Strangely some cultures in Eastern Europe believed it would be lucky to touch Louise Brown, the world's first IVF baby, for the same reason – even though quite clearly her birth was all about science rather than anything supernatural.

In Native American Hopi culture it was Kokopelli who was the fertility God. The happy flute player could help with many things, including having children, and many trinkets, jewelry and drawings were made to help people be blessed with children.

In fact, if you wanted to list all the fertility symbols, stories and traditions there have been over the centuries it would fill another book.

In many office workplaces in the 1970s there was a chair that had the reputation of being the one that you had to use if you wanted to get pregnant. It was passed around or avoided (depending on your feelings) by many secretarial departments and typing pools.

Crystals, including Rose Quartz, have been worn to encourage a baby to arrive; In China elephant statues are said to bring fertility, depending on the positioning of the trunk according to the tradition of feng shui.

Despite the science being available to now help people having problems conceiving many lucky charms still have a huge influence.

In 1993 Ripleys acquired two African fertility statues and since then they have become the all-time most popular Ripley exhibit – and that organization has an awful lot of quirky, interesting and downright weird stuff on display throughout the world.

The statues, which stand five feet high, are supposed to be placed either side of the bedroom door and work their magic if they are touched before entering the bedroom.

The ebony statues were carved by native peoples in the Ivory Coast, Africa, but their powers transferred well to the Ripley Museum in Orlando, Florida where 13 women got pregnant when they came into contact with them.

On world tours since then many couples have sworn that they have "fertility statue babies" born even after being told by doctors they could not have children – or after trying for a long time to start a family. Of course, Ripley have encouraged the publicity – after all it gets people along to their tourist attractions – but there is no doubt the couples are sincere in their beliefs.

Of course, some good luck traditions associated with fertility are rooted in truth. Many foodstuffs – such as pineapple – are said to help encourage pregnancy and nutritionists say there is some level of truth that the anti-inflammatory properties of the foodstuff might help if eaten at the right stage of ovulation.

Fertility doctors do not altogether shy away from the approaches. Most people who present at fertility clinics still have an "unknown cause" of their inability to conceive. Doctors will often conclude that it is the stresses and strains of modern life that are causing some of the difficulties.

Sometimes a good holiday where the couple can relax and get their bodies back into a natural rhythm is all that is needed to do the trick – and positive thinking and believing that a baby will conceive is also part of that style of advice. So, if someone truly believes in their lucky charm it might help get the mindset into the right place for conception.

Of course, many of the ancient fertility symbols are part of the cultural pressure which has through the centuries been put on couples to produce offspring. In many cultures women who did not give birth were criticized, treated as outcasts or made to feel inadequate. Almost always the women took the blame, even if in reality it was the man who had the problem with his sperm.

Kings have removed the heads of wives who did not give them offspring; religious groups have cast out "barren" women so it is no wonder that a lucky charm or anything that might help has been grasped often in desperation by the infertile.

In the very first chapter of the first book of the Bible, mankind is urged by God to "be fruitful and multiply" but the Bible also names women who were "barren" or who struggled to have children.

Now the world of science has opened up a pathway to fertility for many women and men who in the past would not be able to conceive, and with new developments coming along all the time, more and more infertile people who want to have children can source help, without having to resort to superstition. The science is increasing the chances and making "luck" an unnecessary part of the equation.

QUESTIONS

When I was a child of seven or eight years old, I could get away with answering questions without really answering questions. By the time first grade hit, I could effectively dodge a question as well as any politician at the time - and the best part was no one but me knew I was dodging.

It's not a life skill I am proud of, but it has perfected my bullshit detector when it comes to interpersonal interactions.

You see, when I was young, someone could ask me a question about my opinion about the latest technology in the world of fertility treatments and I could simply say something naive like "all I know is that my parents worked really hard to get me here."

And because I was a young, freckle-faced girl, I could get away with that answer. To be honest, I got away with that answer well into my 20s.

I am bluntly honest, and although that's how I have always been with my family and close friends, with the media or perfect strangers, I was always better at hiding my true feelings in some smartly constructed answer that would make them move on to another topic.

And then I had a child myself.

That's when I knew I had to stop dodging.

I dodged questions because I didn't want to offend anyone with my answer. I dodged because I worried I may not sound smart if I got an aspect of the technology wrong (it's not hard to do, by the way, it seems like it is always changing).

I dodged because of the damn pressure I put on myself to be perfect.

Even though my birth was three years after Louise Joy Brown's (the world's first IVF baby), I still felt this enormous pressure growing up that I needed to prove I was normal. I needed to show the world that I was just like every other child.

But the truth is, I wasn't. No person is just like another. That's what makes us human. But I didn't feel that way. I wanted to be so normal that my story was too boring to talk about - make it so reporters said: "she is so much like every other kid out there... we don't have any reason to keep covering her."

It mostly worked.

I was hauled out for major milestones (10 years after I was born, 20 years after I was born, marriage, having a baby...).

And when I did have my son, all I could think was that I didn't want him to wind up with his own Wikipedia page and that I wanted him to be quirky and funny and HIMSELF. Not what he thought he should be for anyone else, but just who he really is.

ANSWERING THE QUESTIONS

The fact that at some time during their lives almost all children question their origins provides a huge challenge for parents who have a child through any of the Assisted Reproductive Technologies or, in fact, anything outside of the natural way.

Being the first meant that Elizabeth Carr knew about her "different" birth from very early days. By the time she was a teenager she had grown tired of hearing about it. But what is it like for a teenager who suddenly discovers that their birth was not all it seemed?

What is the impact if, as a young adult, you learn for the first time that you were IVF? Do you feel some resentment to your parents? Do you feel they have been hiding something from you?

What is the impact if you find out you were born through a surrogate? Maybe that the person who carried you and gave birth to you is someone you have never met? That you were created using sperm, not by the person you have always thought was your father, but a stranger picked out from a list on a computer? What is the likely reaction of someone that learns there was a secret that their parents had never told them?

Every development in the technology has served to make this issue more complex – suddenly discovering that three people were involved in your conception could be quite a shock.

These are major questions that are often talked about in fertility forums; many books have been published to help parents make a choice and decide how and when to tell their child and it is one of the important issues raised by ART and IVF that can not be resolved through science.

It is not really a new issue. Long before IVF came along the families of adopted children faced exactly the same issues and many of the lessons learned in that community have served to help IVF parents as the technology has developed.

Even after 40 years it is still not considered routine to be born through IVF.

Most advice books encourage parents to do exactly what Elizabeth's parents did and tell their child when they are under five years old. The theory is that a child then grows up "never knowing a time" when they didn't know about their conception.

Of course there are also people who, for one reason or another, decide not to say anything and to keep the matter a secret. They also should be respected and supported.

Academic studies have shown that a large number of parents take this route – one study showed up to half of children conceived through egg donation are not told – but in the case of surrogacy almost all children were told. It seems decisions on whether to tell children now vary depending on what kind of Assisted Reproduction took place.

There is now a whole raft of children's story books online for parents to buy and read to their little ones to raise the subject and have that conversation.

Elizabeth was well used to fielding questions about her birth, but for many families, dealing with questions is still a big issue that they need help and support with.

THE TALK

My class was split into two – the boys were sent across the hall while the girls were to remain in our current seats and await the school nurse.

Other than our class being split in two, it was a typical school day for me; struggle through math, relish reading, thrive in writing, get lost in the outlining process in social studies, and royally screw up my science project.

I was almost 11, one of the oldest in my fifth grade class and I was your typical New England preppy: plaid skirts, boat shoes, thick, chunky fall sweaters, and heavy straight across bangs that always seemed to have a cowlick in the front just above my right eyebrow.

I was outspoken and loved to laugh with my classmates.

I was also driven to be an excellent figure skater, taking ice skating lessons before my school day started at a private ice rink a few towns over.

I wanted to be just like Kristy Yamaguchi – she was short and spunky and incredibly talented athletically.

Me?

I was certainly spirited, but my middle name was absolutely not "Grace."

I was (and still am) the girl who tripped up the school stairs on her way back from the lunchroom, who dropped her flute on more than one occasion in after-school music lessons, denting the mouthpiece, and the same girl who had to be rushed to the school nurse's office after getting her finger stuck in said flute while trying to clean the inside of the instrument.

I was also not fast (the irony that I picked up running later in life and have now run countless marathons is still mind boggling to me), and I was consistently picked last in gym class.

In school, there were only a few things that people thought were my redeeming qualities: I could sing (my first singing solo was in first grade), I was a solid writer and storyteller, and I was able to make instant friends with just about anyone – I loved to talk and learn about people.

It's that last quality that tended to get me into trouble with the teachers; they would constantly be moving my seat in the classroom to keep me from chatting with my classmates. I always wondered why they kept moving me, because each new seat was simply a chance to learn about someone new. Hindsight shows they should have kept me in one location and I likely would have eventually gotten bored with my desk-mate.

That morning when the class was split into two, I knew something was up. This was not normal for our class, and the male teachers all were sent across the hall with the boys, while all the female teachers came to our all-girls classroom.

I leaned over to my classmate, nudging her in the ribs with my elbow. "I bet it's 'the talk'," I said to her.

Her eyes opened wide and she gasped back "what talk?"

I rolled my eyes at her.

"You know, the one where they explain all about sex to us…"

I was then promptly interrupted by my classroom teacher "Elizabeth," she said, just giving me THAT look – the one where teachers just want you to be quiet and not cause a stir but they can't actually say that to you, so they just give you THAT look.

"Sorry," I said.

Just as I was turning back to make a face at my classmate, the school nurse entered the room.

"As you get older, your bodies change, ladies," she began.

I knew it.

This was it. This was the sex talk I was thinking it would be.

The school nurse then cued up a video about our "changing bodies" and as I recall it wasn't very riveting, because I'm 99 percent sure I didn't pay attention until the film stopped.

After the video that explained all about hormones and feelings had gone dark, the school nurse went on to explain how men and women come together and have "intercourse" to "create babies".

We were shown a drawing of the uterus and fallopian tubes, and given a worksheet we were to take home that we had colored in of the various parts of the male anatomy as well.

For someone who had the talk about where babies came from when I was quite young, all of this was old hat for me.

So, after the nurse finished her explanation of "how babies are made", she asked for questions.

I looked around the room. There were zero hands in the air.

So, I raised mine.

"Yes, Elizabeth?"

"Well, I know you said that's how babies are made, but that's not at all how I got here," I said matter of factly.

"In my case my mother's egg and my father's sperm were fertilized in a petri dish and then once that happened I went back into my mother's womb and grew like everyone else."

The school nurse didn't know what to say.

And with that, there was a knock on the door from a male

teacher, inquiring if our talk was done and if he could bring the male students back in.

The nurse looked at me, looked around the room and said, "Yes, I don't think we need more time for any more questions."

Being a mother myself now, I am fairly certain that a letter went home from the school to parents of the girls apologizing on my behalf for explaining family building methods outside of the "approved" discussion points previously outlined and approved by the school.

After dinner that night at home with my parents, they asked me (as they always did) how school was, and if I learned anything interesting.

"Well," I said, "I was given this to finish coloring in tonight," as I pulled the worksheet of the male genitalia out and laid it on the dinner table.

My father laughed and my mother glanced at the worksheet, noticing that I had colored part of it in purple and green polka dots.

She looked up at me and said, "well, I certainly hope they told you that if you ever see one that is polka dotted like that, it should be avoided."

Modern Talk

It must have been a shock for a teacher and a school nurse to encounter a child who had not been born in the traditional way as they gave their "birds and bees" talk and to be confronted by the young Elizabeth Carr.

Nothing much had changed in the world of reproduction for thousands of years until IVF came along so the curriculum could stay the same. As well as passing on basic biology most school lessons focused for obvious reasons on telling classes of girls how not to get pregnant.

That meant that many women leaving school and going into the world of full-time education and work were well informed on contraception but unaware about their fertility and how it changes as they get older. Longer university and college courses and the role of women changing so that they wanted to establish themselves in careers or travel before starting a family led to the average age for a first pregnancy rising and the need for fertility help increasing.

Today in almost any USA classroom there is likely to be someone who is only there because of some kind of assisted reproductive technology. How children are informed about the way people reproduce is a matter that needs careful consideration in the 21st century.

Firstly, children born through IVF need to be assured that they are as "normal" as everyone else in the class. It is now a method that has been used for more than 40 years yet many parents worry about whether they should tell their offspring. Most believe it is better to tell them at an early age than for them to find some paperwork years later and say: "why did you never tell me?"

A prompt from a school lesson which tells children there are ways that science can be used to help people conceive can be a catalyst for a discussion in some families.

Secondly, there are now so many other possibilities over the way science helped bring a child into the world. If teachers and school nurses are going to cover these off in full then their discussion about "how babies are made" will need to expand greatly and the boys are going to spend an awful lot of hours in the hall!

So here is a quick run through:

Egg donation: The first successful baby born using an egg donated by another woman dates back to 1984 in Australia. The same year the first US baby using a donated egg was born at the Harbor UCLA Medical Center under the direction of Dr John Buster and the University of California at Los Angeles School of Medicine.

Since 1990 it has been acceptable in the USA to treat age-related infertility using donor eggs, even in women over 40 as long as they are fit enough to carry the baby. Many career women, who maybe had little more than the basic talk in school, have successfully had families this way.

Of course, it throws up some ethical and legal issues and the laws are different in different territories, deciding on when and how egg donation is acceptable. It is illegal in many countries and in others can only be carried out if strict criteria is met.

Now, thanks to egg banks and slick techniques, it is possible for a woman who does not produce healthy eggs to have a baby using an egg donated by another woman, depending on other medical factors. More controversially, in some people's views, it can be used to enable a woman to have a baby with a donated egg rather than passing on a genetic disorder that they are aware of in their own eggs.

Egg donation may also be part of the journey for same-sex male couples starting a family. Statistics seem to suggest that around 5% of all IVF births worldwide are now through donated eggs with tens of thousands of US children born using this technique and likely to put up their hands and ask an awkward question in a talk!

Cryogenic techniques: In 1986 obstetrician Christopher Chen was the first to successfully freeze a human egg. The technique has led to a whole industry revolving around preserving good quality eggs that can then be used later in life.

There are now over 500,000 human eggs stored in the USA as many people use the technique as a lifestyle choice to enable them to have a baby later in life from a healthy egg removed when they were younger.

Of course freezing eggs was originally developed to provide vital support for women with serious conditions such as Cancer, where chemotherapy and other treatments can lead to infertility. It means that diagnosis does not necessarily mean that they also have to resign themselves to a lifetime of being childless.

Different techniques have been developed and debated over the years and in common with every step taken in fertility treatment legal and moral issues mean that the rules are different all over the world. How long eggs can be frozen and still remain useable has also become a major debate – in 2012 a woman in Argentina successfully gave birth to twins using eggs that had been stored for 12 years.

Fertilizing the eggs and freezing the embryos was the next step with Zoe Leyland of Australia being the world's first baby born from a frozen embryo in 1984. Major work in the USA and the Netherlands on techniques for both freezing and thawing of eggs and embryos have led to many more options open to in this developing procedure.

Certainly, children born as a result of cryogenically freezing eggs can have some fun with their teachers – they could be twins born years apart, for instance!

Surrogacy: In the 1980s many thousands of newspaper columns were taken up with debating the rights and wrongs of surrogacy, where a woman carries another woman's baby for her. IVF made it possible for gestational surrogacy, where volunteer surrogates receive an embryo and give birth to a couple's baby in circumstances where a woman could not carry the baby herself.

But famous legal cases, such as that involving Baby M, went on for years, as the arrangements for just how legally and morally such arrangements could work. Today, surrogacy is commonly used by same sex couples in some jurisdictions, is highly controlled in other jurisdictions and is banned completely in others.

There is no Federal Law regarding surrogacy. In 46 US states gestational surrogacy is recognized and in four US states it is illegal (New York, Nebraska, Michigan and Louisiana). Across the world it is equally complicated – in the UK and Belgium for example it is legal but the surrogate can not be paid more than "reasonable expenses". In neighboring France it is illegal.

High profile surrogate births, such as the sons of Elton John and David Furnish in California, have served to fuel the debate. So, in some states teacher may come across a child who says their birth mother is not the same as the one raising them!

Elizabeth's birth and the development of IVF have certainly given some interesting conundrums for teachers trying to work out the "sex talk" of the future.

ASKING FOR TIME OFF

My search for a college was very different from the stories my friends told me. Their versions included making a list of places they wanted to go, deciding when to visit them, poring for hours over their college application essays and waiting with bated breath for a response.

Me? I tagged along on a road trip to a few schools two of my buddies were interested in. We piled into the back of an old Saab (I sat on the hump between my two longer-legged male friends) and saw Ithaca College (known for a solid communications program) and Eastman (an elite music school).

It was colder than cold when we visited, and when I learned that it snowed more in upstate New York than it did in Massachusetts, I wrote both schools off my list.

I wasn't really gung-ho in my college search, so my father suggested one day that I attend a free course at Simmons College in Boston on "how to write your college essay."

It sounded downright boring, but I figured maybe I could muster up the motivation to write a really compelling essay (that quite frankly I didn't care one bit about writing).

The day of the course, the first thing I had to do that day was find a bathroom. I had ingested far too much coffee on the way into the city and now was paying for it. As I was washing my hands, I glanced down and saw freshly cut flowers.

"Nice touch," I thought.

Next, I found my way to the lecture hall and grabbed a seat in the middle of the room. A bunch of girls filtered in behind me and also grabbed seats. Our parents were off in another room. Then, it happened.

Professor David Gullette entered the room. His voice wasn't loud, and he wasn't particularly tall, but he captivated us all.

He spoke about writing this college essay as if it were some form of poetry about ourselves, "a vehicle to show complete strangers the marrow of your being."

He used catch phrases like "MEEGO" (My eyes glazed over) and at one point actually had us laughing.

If this man could make me laugh about writing something I had absolutely NO interest in writing about before entering that room, I figured I should probably figure out what class he taught at Simmons and just what I had to do in order to occupy a seat there.

I applied early action to Simmons, having simply to fill out a shortened application, did not have to write a college essay, and simply had to have one in-person interview before I was officially the FIRST member of the class of 2004.

He taught Shakespeare -- a class available only to upper class women. I spoke to my advisor, and basically begged to get into the class – as a freshman. I told Professor Gullette he would not regret it, to which I remember him responding "I have no doubt."

I got an A in his class.

That first semester at Simmons pretty much set me up as a student who liked to take on challenges – who would tackle what looked like the hardest task and relish how hard it was. I loved being told something I wanted to do was "too difficult" or impossible.

So, in my freshman year I tackled Shakespeare, then my sophomore year I really had to reach. I decided to apply for a co-op position at The Boston Globe, after taking just one journalism 101 course with a then Boston Globe columnist.

Once again, Simmons had never had anyone so young apply for such a thing, and they approved my application with the caveat that I still needed to carry a full course load.

I agreed.

So, there I was, a sophomore in college with almost NO published clips to her name other than her college paper, working as an obituary writer for The Boston Globe (during the height of the Spotlight series on the scandals at the Catholic church). I was working 40 hours a week at the Globe, lifeguarding at the college pool before my shifts at the Globe, and then loading up my schedule with every evening class Simmons offered at the time so that I could get my full four courses in.

To say that I had established myself as a hard-worker would be somewhat of an understatement. But, let's face it – I was still only a sophomore in college, which comes with all kinds of connotations and baggage.

One day, while working out in one of the Globe's bureau offices, I was reminded by my parents that I needed to get time off from the Globe in order to deliver a speech.

Back then, co-ops did not get time off, so I was extremely nervous about asking my managers, Carol and Shirley, for two days off.

I remember sitting in a chair in front of both of their desks just waiting for them to pepper me with questions – as all good editors do.

"What do you need the time off for?" Carol asked.

"I'm giving a speech at the United Nations," I said.

Carol cracked a smile and glanced over at Shirley with a look that I could only imagine meant, "Yeah right, she's giving a speech at the U.N."

"I think the Globe was sending a photographer, actually," I told Carol.

"Ok, sure, see you when you get back," she said.

The next time I was in the office, we didn't discuss my trip to New York, and at the end of my co-op Carol and another editor offered me to stay on longer.

Years later, during my goodbye party for leaving the Globe after 15 years, Carol cornered me. "Remember when you asked for time off for a speech? I didn't believe you because I had heard all kinds of excuses from kids, but your speech made the paper the next day."

I still have a hard time asking for time off to attend or speak at infertility events.

I always think my bosses will think I'm just making this whole "test tube" thing up.

TIME OFF FOR THE UN

Donald Trump, Barack Obama, JFK, Colin Powell, Fidel Castro, Muammar Gadaffi, Nelson Mandela and Elizabeth Carr are just some of the people who have given a speech at the United Nations. Can you spot the odd one out?

We all hear about the major role that the United Nations plays when there is conflict in the world but it was set up after the Second World War to do more than referee on war and peace.

Its charter states that its aim is "to achieve international co-operation in solving international problems of an economic, social, cultural, or humanitarian character".

Issues thrown up by IVF fit perfectly into this role as countries across the world had to come to terms with the new possibilities, learn from each other's breakthroughs and decide how the new fertility treatment fitted into the ethics and laws of each culture.

As each new innovation in Assisted Reproductive Technology has been developed it has had the possibility to change the whole demographic of countries and that too is a vital area for the UN to keep tabs on.

Will bringing more people into the world mean there isn't enough food to go around? Will some cultures use the technology in a way not acceptable to others? How does fertility treatment impact on poor economies or better off countries? These are big global questions.

The United Nations Population Division was founded in 1946. It looks at three main areas that affect the population of countries fertility, mortality and immigration. It regularly publishes a "World Fertility Report" that crunches the numbers on people being born across the world, age of parents and other issues affecting fertility.

The reports show that there was a post war baby boom but in the 1970s there were the first signs of levels of population taking a different trend. Some 22 countries across the world in the 1970s reported numbers that showed that the number of babies being born was lower than that needed to replace the population – so populations were falling.

Despite the invention of IVF at the end of that decade and other advances in fertility treatment the UN reported that by 2013 the number of countries with below replacement fertility had almost quadrupled to 83, not only that but half the world's population lived in those 83 countries.

These population trends also meant that there was a greater number of older people and less younger people to care for them.

All major issues affecting the future of the world – IVF and the views of those involved in it and other Assisted Reproductive Techniques are important elements in that mix that the United Nations needs to continue to consider.

HUMAN LIFE

I sat staring at the beige carpet on the floor of my parents'
bedroom through hot tears silently streaming down my face.
They weren't tears of anger or sadness. Instead, they were
tears of relief.

Finally, I thought, someone had recognized that my life was
going to be, well, different. The tears were brought on by a letter.

I discovered it in a scrapbook at the bottom of one of the
closets in my parents' bedroom. I started snooping in the closet
when I spied their wedding album.

I was 10, and was drawn to the retro-styles my parents were
wearing. After flipping through the wedding album, I found
more photo albums – one of which was filled with candid family
snapshots from the time right before I was born.

It was Christmas. Mom was decorating a small, fake tree with
petite colored lights and red velvet bows. She was in a maternity
dress, her face beaming with happiness. What held my attention
to that photograph, though, at the time, wasn't the joy in her
face: Instead it was the fact that the woman was wearing three
inch heels at nine months pregnant.

The next page contained more photos – this time of Dad
opening an antique level and bottle of cologne. And then I spied

something tucked between the pages.

It was a 12 page letter, written in blue ink.

All caps.

The printing was neat and straight. It was on unlined paper, so I caught myself, at times, wondering how he kept the lines of text so perfectly straight.

Dr. Fredrick Wirth was the neonatologist on staff the day I was born in Virginia. It was his job to determine my score on the ever-important Apgar test, and his job to tell the rest of the team of doctors his assessment of if I was a "normal, healthy" baby or not.

I had seen Dr. Wirth before in the NOVA documentary of my birth: he was the man who carried me out of the delivery room. He had me wrapped in a blanket and tucked under his arm as if he were carrying a football going in for a touchdown: snug, tight.

He was wearing a hospital mask though in the documentary, so I had only ever seen his eyes, piercing bluish gray. Like a wolf.

That day, on the floor of my parents' bedroom, my 10-year-old mind got to know a bit about Dr. Wirth. This man had taken it upon himself in the hours shortly after my birth to sit down and write me a letter (he left instructions with my parents to have me read the letter when I was old enough to understand my origins).

"You are special, Elizabeth," he wrote. "But not because of how you were born. Because of how much your parents love you, and wanted you. You are special because you are theirs."

That paragraph sticks with me to this day, and I have actually told people interviewing me that exact quote, stealing it from Dr. Wirth as my own.

Dr. Wirth was the only person who helped me really understand what my parents went through emotionally, and physically, without laying out the gory details involved in the medical procedures, or the mundane details about just how frequently they flew back and forth between Virginia and Massachusetts just for my mother's check-ups.

Dr. Wirth left the hospital in Virginia shortly after my birth, so I never ran into him at annual reunions, and he never greeted my parents and I when we came to visit.

It always bothered me that this man whose words meant so much to me, I had never formally met, and that I had only seen half of his face in a documentary.

When I was an intern at the Virginian-Pilot newspaper in Norfolk, Virginia, I told one of my editors about Dr. Wirth. One of them asked me if I had ever tried to track him down. I was, my editor reminded me, an adept reporter who could find a needle in a haystack if I needed to.

My editor was right. I could. What had taken me so long to try?

I made up my mind to find Dr. Wirth.

In my head, I started calling him Fred. I did Google searches. Searched public records in Virginia. Scoured medical licenses in various states. I went to the motor vehicle registry. I looked to see if he filed for bankruptcy. If there was a public record out there, I searched it for his name.

Finally, after about a month, I came across a website for a clinic in Pennsylvania and, it turned out, my man Fred had just published a book - and the jacket flap mentioned he was the neonatologist for the first 'test tube baby' in the U.S.

That's my man, I thought.

I studied the picture on the book flap. It was in black and white, but he still had the same piercing eyes. I sent an e-mail using the contact form on his website, since I couldn't find a phone number. And then, I waited.

Months went by. My summer internship ended. My e-mail to Fred went unanswered.

I was disappointed I may never meet the doctor in person. In a way, I felt like I was missing a piece of myself I needed to know about, and somehow, it involved meeting him.

And then one day, I got an e-mail back. Dr. Wirth told me that my e-mail had gotten stuck in a spam filter, but that he would absolutely love to meet, and asked if he could come to Boston to see me.

He told me my e-mail made his day, because I had thanked him, something, he said, neonatologists rarely hear even though they are often the first people to take care of a newborn. We exchanged a flurry of e-mails.

I called my parents. Dr. Wirth and I spoke over the phone, and set up our meeting in Boston.

A newspaper reporter was on hand to document our first hug.

"I've saved hundreds of children's lives, and none of them have bothered to even call me. I'm overwhelmed," he told the reporter.

I was overwhelmed that day, too - mostly because for one of the first times in my life, I didn't know what to say.

So, I started by telling him the story of sitting on my parents' floor, and bawling my eyes out.

DR FREDERICK WIRTH

Dr Frederick Wirth, who died in 2009 at the age of 68, is one of a whole raft of "unsung heroes" or "best supporting actors" that worked alongside the pioneers of IVF.

It was reported that he cared for around 100,000 babies during his career but it was a special moment when he was handed baby Elizabeth after a caesarean section on her mother Judy at 7.46am on December 28, 1981.

It was Dr Wirth who carried out all the checks to ensure the baby was "normal" and "healthy". It was a tense moment for the team as there had been a few issues spotted on scans during the pregnancy.

Later when the press gathered in a conference room he didn't stick to the script but instead declared Elizabeth was "a wonderful baby".

Just as Neil Armstrong, Buzz Aldrin and Michael Collins will always be the first names associated with conquering the Moon, so will Howard and Georgeanna Jones be the names that live on in bringing IVF to America. But in both cases there were a lot of people in Mission Control that made it happen!

Wirth's words in that letter to Elizabeth resonate with many patient groups that now exist where those going through IVF look for support on whether they should tell their children they were not born naturally – and how, and at what age, to do that.

It is certainly true that every IVF baby can be absolutely sure they were wanted and not an "accident" and that their parents went through a lot to bring them into the world. That message works today just as much as it did when Dr Wirth wrote it down in 1981.

In recent years there has been a movement to recognise some of those lesser-known figures in the pioneering days of IVF. One such person is Jean Purdy. She worked with Robert Edwards and Patrick Steptoe and was effectively the world's first IVF nurse and embryologist.

While Steptoe and Edwards had gone home to their families she stayed on to watch the cells dividing in the petri dish that were eventually to become Louise Brown, so witnessed first-hand the first IVF success.

Sadly, she died aged just 39 in 1985 but a new headstone was placed on her grave in Grantchester, England, to mark her importance in the process around the 40th anniversary of those events. Anyone who watches the birth on YouTube will see the eminent doctors pull Jean Purdy into the frame as they saw her as a vital part of the crew. Another worthy of mention is John Webster, who had the same role at Louise Brown's birth as Dr Wirth had at Elizabeth Carr's.

Fertility treatment is always a team effort and Dr Frederick Wirth was a vital part of the team in Norfolk, Virginia that made history. His letter to Elizabeth shows just how much he realised that this was not just another medical procedure – it was creating a human life.

BIG FAMILY

As a sophomore in High School I begged my parents to host an exchange student for half the year.

"Come on," I said. "I've never had a brother or sister, so just let me do this."

I don't know if it was my incessant begging, or the fact that my parents thought it would be a good experience for me, but whatever it was they eventually gave in.

Zhenya was from Moscow. She was very sweet, but we had virtually nothing in common (except the fact that we were both living at my house), and although I did pick up some Russian words and phrases, it made me realize that I was not cut out to share my parents.

I was destined to be an only child, I think.

I had an adult sense of humor as a five-year-old and could hold my own in heady discussions about politics with my parents' friends when I hit my teens.

I always wanted a big family when I was a child. I thought it would be so awesome to have built-in playmates.

Because of that, my house was always the house where everyone congregated as I got older.

My parents bought root beer by the gallon jug and stocked up on tea they never drank just so my friends and I could take over the living room, sprawled on the carpet laughing and making fun of each other.

It was not unusual to find a friend or two of mine waiting for me to get home, sitting in my kitchen, having coffee with my mom.

My friends have always been my family since my actual relatives live all across the country.

In school my friends were the people I played field hockey with, or whom sang with me in choir. They were the boy down the street, and the girl who sat next to me in class.

In college, my rowing teammates were the people who held me together, bonding over waking up to run three miles to our boathouse, row six miles, and run three back all before we had even consumed breakfast.

Running though, running is the one place I've managed to find that big family I wanted when I was a kid.

A run with a friend can heal any bad day, a RUNch with other friends for giggles, early morning miles with my husband, or foggy miles next to the river with my running teammate, runs past Starbucks with girlfriends, chatty miles with my son, running "just one more" with my marathon training partners…

Running always feels like home.

Running has always been the place I can pretend I have a big family, all united behind a single goal.

BIG FAMILIES

Many people want a big family – and some end up with them all at once! The increased use of drugs for fertility treatment and the invention of IVF led to a surge in multiple births, especially in the early days of the technology when failure rates were higher than they are today so it was felt that transferring a number of embryos back into the womb would increase the chances of success.

The problem was that if they were all successful the mother could end up with a lot of little mouths to feed all at once, and the chances of survival of the babies fighting for space in the womb and invariably being born under-weight were reduced.

Of course, multiple births had always happened. Twins and triplets have been reported throughout history and back in 1934 the Dionne Quintuplets, born in Callander, Ontario, Canada were the first known survival of five children.

Their birth was as big a sensation as that of Elizabeth Carr. The five children, all girls, were born two months premature and weighed just 2lb each. They were cared for in a specially created hospital opposite their parents farmhouse, that was dubbed "Quintland".

Tourists queued to pay to go in and look at the five girls and, as they grew, observation areas were set up for the tourists to look at them in their outdoor play area! The local gas station did such good business that it had five pumps installed and named them after each of the five girls – Emilie, Marie, Annette, Yvonne and Cecile.

Around three million tourists visited the nursery between 1936 and 1943 – more than visited the Canadian side of Niagra Falls and making them Canada's biggest tourist attraction with a whole souvenir trade growing up around them.

The exploitation of the children shows just some of the dangers that can happen from multiple births.

Multiple births as a result of fertility treatment pre-dates Elizabeth and IVF. Modern fertility treatment really began in 1958 with successful ovulation induction techniques developed by Sweden's Dr Carl Gemzell using pituitary-derived gonadotropins.

The ovulation drug Pergonal was introduced in 1963 and by 1965 Life Magazine was reporting a "multiple birth epidemic"

Stimulation drugs are often used in conjunction with IVF treatment. The percentage of triplets and twins as a proportion of total births has increased dramatically since IVF but even with fertility drugs 80% of births are of single babies. However, there are many more multiple births among those undergoing IVF than among those conceiving naturally.

With more sophisticated techniques and informed legislation fertility treatment has become more accurate and so much more can now be done before implantation to ensure that the embryo will develop successfully into a baby.

Multiple births have been, and remain, an issue for the fertility world to tackle. The cost on health services, the financial difficulties that families face trying to cope with multiple births and the increased danger to the baby if they are born underweight all have to be factored in.

The Centers for Disease Control and Prevention showed that in 1980, one in every 53 babies born in the USA was a twin – by 2005 this had grown to one in every 30. The figures show that multiple births as a result of ART increased from 1983 to 2005. Since then the per centage number has rapidly decreased

Elizabeth's birth sparked a period of instant big families in the USA and around the world. She may not have had a big family but the industry that she represents has contributed to creating many.

GRATEFUL

I am not ungrateful for the life I have had.

Every day I am grateful I am here. I am grateful to so many people – doctors, nurses, my parents, anonymous donors who gave money to start the IVF clinic where I was born…

Grateful does not seem sufficient a word most days.

Other days I just feel… awkward.

I feel awkward when people ask me why I was born in Virginia rather than Massachusetts (because IVF was illegal in Mass. at the time)

I feel awkward when people ask me if I have siblings (my mother was lucky to have one egg that worked).

When people ask "why didn't you TELL me you were the FIRST IVF baby" (because it's not something that one can just bring up within the first sentence of meeting someone – do you talk about how you were born on a first date?)

When parents ask me how my parents told me I was an IVF baby and how and when they should tell their own children (I feel like I've known since I was born simply because the press has been in my life since I was three cells old (yes, cells) and it is up to each parent as to what they want to do and what they think is best for their child. That is a personal decision and there is no guidebook or rule. I will say, learning about my birth early in life did make learning sex education a heck of a lot easier.

I feel awkward when people want my autograph. I am always flattered but I seriously didn't do anything. I just showed up. I will never say no, however, because I also understand what it means to this community to be able to talk openly, honestly, and fearlessly about IVF and other reproductive technologies.

But awkward, I have learned, is OK. Because no moment that matters is quite comfortable.

FUTURE HOPE

At every stage of my childhood, I can remember thinking how far reproductive technology and options have come.

I remember holding the first set of twins birthed at the clinic where I was born.

I remember getting a tour of one of the first stateside facilities to cryo-preserve (or freeze) women's eggs.

I remember discussions of preimplantation genetic testing taking place at medical conferences when it was still nothing more than hypothetical rather than reality.

But, as far as we've come, there's always more work to be done.

As of the writing of this book, only 19 states in the U.S. have passed laws that require insurers to either cover or offer coverage for infertility diagnosis and treatment. Of those states, only 15 have laws that require insurance companies to cover infertility treatments, and two states – California and Texas – have laws that require companies to offer coverage for infertility treatment.

We can – and should – do better.

Additionally, each year I still am told by many people trying to create a family that the stigma and silence surrounding fertility issues has not improved.

There are so many groups, organizations, and foundations out there doing good work, but so many people still don't know about the resources available to them. Why?

Collectively, we have to raise resources that are critical to those in need. We must continue to fight for more insurance coverage, more access, more discussion.

We cannot take our foot off of the gas pedal now, not when so many need us to continue the charge ahead.

My hope is that some day all available reproductive options will be covered during sex-ed discussions in schools, so that there isn't one single child raising her hand saying "not all babies are born that way."

We are not alone in this fight.

SPONSOR REFLECTIONS

This book has been made possible thanks to the backing of Brown Fertility, Nikon Instruments and Genomic Prediction. The following articles outline how they link to Elizaberth's story.

Brown Fertility
CONCEIVING MIRACLES™

THE IVF REVOLUTION
Brown Fertility

Forty years ago the world was an entirely different place. Abroad, Cold War tensions ran high with the Iron Curtain still in place and the Middle East in turmoil.

In the United States, the impending arrival of the first "test tube" baby and the uncertainty of the outcome was causing uproars and tremors alike. Mass demonstrations and rioting were taking place over the fears of a potential, "IVF Baby Frankenstein."

In fact, two speeches had been drafted in the event that the birth of an "abnormal" or a "normal" baby had been created from this new fertility treatment called IVF.

By the grace of God and science a normal, healthy beautiful baby was born - Elizabeth Carr - thanks to the perseverance of pioneering physicians Drs. Howard and Georgeanna Jones of the Jones Institute for Reproductive Medicine in Norfolk, Virginia, and Elizabeth's parents, an infertile couple desperate to have a family. I myself completed my Reproductive Endocrinology and Infertility Fellowship at the prestigious Jones Institute and all of us who were mentored by these pioneers knew something remarkable had taken place.

As I walked the halls two decades after the birth of Elizabeth Carr, her successful birth was sensed a colossal scientific medical moment moving, us into a new era of scientific-based medical fertility treatment.

Elizabeth's birth, touted on front pages all over the world, became a modern medical miracle and represented hope to millions of Americans with infertility.

We have since made incredible strides to incorporate IVF into our normal daily lives. I'm humbly honored to have this special connection to Elizabeth. Given the limitless potential of reproductive medicine, as the youngest form of medicine, 40 years doesn't seem that long ago.

We are still at the forefront of a revolution.

By Samuel E. Brown, MD, Founder & Medical Director of Brown Fertility

ELIZABETH CARR AND MICROSCOPY:
A MATCH MADE IN THE COSMOS
Nikon

O ver the last 40 years, millions of couples have become parents with the help of in vitro fertilization (IVF); yet, what many people don't know is that this process was pioneered using a Nikon Diaphot TMD microscope by Drs. Howard and Georgeanna Jones, resulting in the birth of Elizabeth Carr. Since then, a wave of fertilization techniques and biotechnology have provided hope and opportunity for couples who previously were unable to conceive.

At Nikon, we have had the honor of occasionally being a part of Elizabeth's life – beginning with playing a part in how she entered the world, and later in her adult life when she came to Nikon and participated as an honorary judge and distinguished guest in the Nikon Small World Competition. This competition is widely regarded as the leading forum to honor visual excellence in video and photography through the microscope. When Elizabeth joined our judging panel, it was a symbolic moment for us. The mere sight of her interacting with leading scientists and journalists showed at that moment that the human experience knows no bounds. Her life, and the many lives that began using IVF, are a testament to the power of science to change our lives and the world.

The Expanding Universe of IVF Technology Breakthroughs

Since 1981, Nikon has played a significant role in the development and advancement of IVF techniques. Today, a new generation of IVF methods have emerged, such as ICSI (intracytoplasmic sperm injection), PGS/D (preimplantation genetic screening/diagnosis) and IMSI (intracytoplasmic morphology selected sperm injection). All rely on microscopy for success, and all have advanced the science for better human health and outcomes.

Through the years, these scientific achievements have helped reduce the number of multiple pregnancies, and improved success rates. For patients experiencing infertility or otherwise are unable to conceive, IVF has proven to be a viable option in achieving a healthy pregnancy and a healthy child. While other assisted reproduction technology is effective, IVF can help diagnose fertilization challenges and allow couples to screen for inherited diseases. IVF also allows for single women and same sex couples to become parents as well, making what once seemed impossible, possible.

Today's instruments are designed to minimize cells' environmental stress and optimize their viability during imaging, thereby providing embryos with the best possible start in life. This is important for clinics, but also vital in reducing the emotional stress and financial cost to patients.

A Look Ahead

There are so many lessons in Elizabeth's story. Lessons of perseverance and joy, of hope and resilience, of science and possibility. We're honored to be recognized for the small part we played in her story. Of course, the scientists and medical professionals involved at that time, and those who have led the way in developing new techniques for fertility treatment, rightly deserve the praise.

At the same time, when we take a close look at the tools and technologies supporting them, it takes a phenomenal collaborative and supported effort to make life-changing advances. To know that Nikon technologies have helped to lay the foundation that has given joy to millions of parents around the world fills us with humility and gratitude.

About Nikon Microscopes Utilized in IVF

Nikon microscope imaging systems include upright microscopes, inverted systems for live cell imaging, stereo microscopes, digital imaging equipment and, most recently, the BioStation, a combined incubation and imaging system. The most current IVF offering from Nikon, the ECLIPSE Ti2-U IVF (EU/US), provides an ultra-stable platform for performing precision manipulation procedures such as ICSI. Its intermediate magnification switching function (1.5X) allows easy switching of observation magnification without changing objectives.

Along with a comprehensive range of microscopes for IVF, Nikon also supplies high tech microscope imaging systems and analysis software to enhance a vast range of scientific research endeavors. From IVF to cancer and Alzheimer's research, these tools, fostered by optical techniques and digital imaging technologies, have enabled scientists to greatly advance their impact on human life.

At Nikon, we understand that science can be more than just discovery. Science changes lives and Elizabeth's book is a living testament to the degree in which that impact can be felt. From someone who literally owes her existence to the collaboration of scientific communities and technologies, we at Nikon are proud to play a small part in this noble quest.

FERTILITY FIRSTS CONTINUE
LifeView by Genomic Prediction

The first baby in history to be conceived via polygenic selection was born in the summer of 2020.

She was the first in a new generation, growing rapidly, of IVF embryos chosen via polygenic screening. These embryo choices are leading to pregnancies, and to the births of many more babies like her.

It's done as part of the normal IVF process, added to now-standard Down Syndrome testing. No extra risks or procedures.

Screening of embryos has been happening since the early 1990s. But until 2019, it has been confined to disorders passed on via single genes or "Monogenic" disorders.

In 2019, Genomic Prediction Clinical Laboratory performed history's first polygenic screen: PGT-P. The acronym stands for Preimplantation Genetic Testing for "Polygenic" disorders.

Type 1 Diabetes, Coronary Artery Disease, Breast Cancer, and Schizophrenia are on the growing list of what can be screened. All are screened in parallel, reducing the risk of the whole list at the same time.

PGT-P is a significant improvement over PGT-M, or testing for Monogenic disorders, like BRCA1 - a gene which famously increases the risk of breast cancer. BRCA1 is powerful, but it's rare. It only causes 5% of breast cancer. The more advanced

PGT-P method is now addressing the other 95%. It reduces breast cancer risk (and other cancer risks) in everyone. Not just the few with a rare gene, like BRCA1.

This is a game changer. It has implications for the health of everyone, equally as important as those which prompted the birth of Elizabeth in 1982. But not everyone is happy about it.

Elizabeth Carr's birth led to criticism from many groups. Debates about ethics, about safety. Legislators across the USA and the world were rushing to the statute books, deciding whether the technology should be banned. Today, IVF is global, and commonplace. It has changed the nature of childbirth, and even the nature of family itself. It's astonishing how much thinking has changed.

The nightmare scenarios that those opposed to IVF had have not come to pass. Today, one out of 10 Danish babies are born via IVF every year. And the rest of the world is quickly catching up.

One couple who have gone through PGT-P screening, but wanted to remain anonymous, tell their story. They sourced a surrogate to carry the baby. They had another woman donate eggs. They went through the legal hoops, and found an IVF clinic. And crucially, they had a family history of breast cancer, but no monogenic disorder like BRCA1 to screen against. So, they took the extra step to cut the risk of their child having breast cancer, as well as various other disorders known to be in their families.

In April 2019, a total of 33 of their healthy embryos were screened by Genomic Prediction. From the PGT-P reports, they chose the embryo that was to become their future child.

The first baby born from an embryo selected after polygenic screening is Aurea Smigrodzki. Her father, medical doctor Rafal Smigrodzki, wanted the child to have risk mitigation on every disease available on the PGT-P panel, though he was particularly interested in heart disease.

He said: "Aurea's smile tells you more about the importance of this screening than any words from me. This is about doing everything we can for her."

Professor Simon Fishel, UK physiologist and biochemist, worked alongside Patrick Steptoe and Nobel-laureate Bob Edwards, whose work led to the birth of Louise Brown, the first IVF baby. He believes the PGT-P screening could have implications for the world just the way the first IVF births did.

"I see so many parallels with the work of Edwards and Steptoe," says Fishel. "I know from working alongside them that they could not have imagined the extent of the changes that have resulted from their work. I firmly believe that if Edwards and Steptoe had not met, then IVF would have taken another 10 years. At Genomic Prediction, you have a similar meeting of minds that has led to this breakthrough. Edwards even predicted PGT-P, back in '93. I'm sure he would be working with us today, if he were here."

Fishel sees a new normal where polygenic screening becomes routine.

Genomic Prediction's Chief Science Officer and Cofounder, Dr. Nathan Treff, said: "We want to make PGT-P available to anyone interested in selecting among their embryos. Especially if either they themselves, or family members, have been diagnosed with polygenetic conditions.

"I have Type 1 diabetes myself. The ability to mitigate risk of passing it on to your own child is something that every parent should have." Genomic Prediction's test for Type 1 diabetes was the first the company published, showing they can select among siblings from the same family to reduce disease risk by over 70%, validating it on 3,000 families. Later PGT-P tests were proven on 10x more families.

"Why leave your child's health to chance? Choice is better." Laurent Tellier, the company's CEO and Cofounder, said. "Everyone can give their child the best possible start."